FOX

BY ADRIENNE RICH

Arts of the Possible: Essays and Conversations

Midnight Salvage: Poems 1995–1998

Dark Fields of the Republic: Poems 1991–1995

Collected Early Poems 1950–1970

An Atlas of the Difficult World: Poems 1988–1991

Time's Power: Poems 1985–1988

Blood, Bread, and Poetry: Selected Prose 1979–1985

Your Native Land, Your Life: Poems

The Fact of a Doorframe: Poems Selected and New 1950–1984

Sources

A Wild Patience Has Taken Me This Far: Poems 1978–1981

On Lies, Secrets, and Silence: Selected Prose 1966–1978

The Dream of a Common Language: Poems 1974–1977

Twenty-one Love Poems

Of Woman Born: Motherhood as Experience and Institution

Poems: Selected and New, 1950–1974

Diving into the Wreck: Poems 1971–1972

The Will to Change

Leaflets

Necessities of Life

Snapshots of a Daughter-in-Law

The Diamond Cutters

A Change of World

FOX

POEMS 1998–2000

ADRIENNE RICH

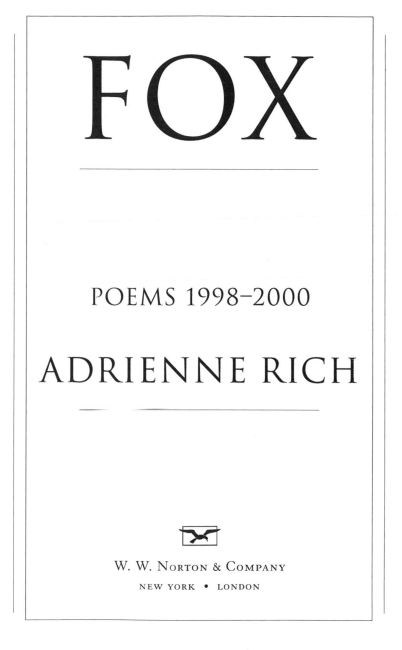

W. W. NORTON & COMPANY

NEW YORK • LONDON

For information about permission to reproduce selections from this book,
write to Permissions, W. W. Norton & Company, Inc., 500 Fifth Avenue,
New York, NY 10110.

The text of this book is composed in Granjon,
with the display set in Trajan.
Book design by Brooke Koven.
Manufacturing by Courier Companies, Inc.
Production manager: Leelo Märjamaa-Reintal.

Library of Congress Cataloging-in-Publication Data

Rich, Adrienne Cecile.
    Fox : poems 1998–2000 / by Adrienne Rich.
      p. cm.
    ISBN 0-393-04166-2
    I. Title.

PS3535.I233 F69   2001
811'.54—dc21

                                                        2001031240

W. W. Norton & Company, Inc., 500 Fifth Avenue, New York, N.Y. 10110
www.wwnorton.com

W. W. Norton & Company Ltd., Castle House, 75/76 Wells Street, London
W1T 3QT

            1   2   3   4   5   6   7   8   9   0

My appreciation to the journals where these poems first appeared:
Connect, Doubletake, Fence, Paris Review,
Poetry International, Sulfur, The American Poetry Review,
The Progressive, The Radcliffe Quarterly

For Michelle, again,
after twenty-five years

Y in alto cielo, su fondo estrellado
Y en las multitudes, la mujer que amo

CONTENTS

FOX

VICTORY

Something spreading underground won't speak to us
under skin won't declare itself
not all life-forms want dialogue with the
machine-gods in their drama   hogging down
the deep bush   clear-cutting refugees
from ancient or transient villages into
our opportunistic fervor   to search
                    crazily for a host   a lifeboat

Suddenly instead of art we're eyeing
organisms traced and stained on cathedral transparencies
cruel blues   embroidered purples   succinct yellows
a beautiful tumor

I guess you're not alone   I fear you're alone
There's, of course, poetry:
awful bridge rising over naked air: I first
took it as just a continuation of the road:
"a masterpiece of engineering
praised, etc."   then on the radio:
"incline too steep for ease of, etc."
Drove it nonetheless because I had to
this being how—   So this is how
I find you: alive and more

As if (how many conditionals must we suffer?)
I'm driving to your side
—an intimate collusion—
packed in the trunk my bag of foils for fencing with pain
glasses of varying spectrum for sun or fog or sun-struck
                       rain or bitterest night my sack of hidden
poetries, old glue shredding from their spines

my time exposure of the Leonids
                         over Joshua Tree

As if we're going to win this   O because

If you have a sister I am not she
nor your mother nor you my daughter
nor are we lovers or any kind of couple
    except in the intensive care
                      of poetry and
death's master plan   architecture-in-progress
draft elevations of a black-and-white mosaic dome
the master left on your doorstep
with a white card in black calligraphy:
    Make what you will of this
    As if leaving purple roses

If (how many conditionals must we suffer?)
I tell you a letter from the master
is lying on my own doorstep
glued there with leaves and rain
and I haven't bent to it yet
                    if I tell you I surmise
    he writes differently to me:

        Do as you will, you have had your life
        many have not

signing it in his olden script:

    Meister aus Deutschland

In coldest Europe   end of that war
frozen domes   iron railings frozen   stoves lit in the
    streets
memory banks of cold

the Nike of Samothrace
on a staircase   wings in blazing
backdraft   said to me
: : to everyone she met
        Displaced, amputated   never discount me

Victory
        indented in disaster   striding
            at the head of stairs

for Tory Dent

1998

VETERANS DAY

1

No flag heavy or full enough to hide this face
this body swung home from home   sewn into its skin

Let you   entrusted to close the box
for final draping   take care

what might be due
to the citizen wounded

by no foreign blast nor shell   *(is this
body a child's?   if?   why?)*

eyes hooded in refusal—
over these to lower the nation's pall, thick flutter

this body shriveled into itself
—a normal process they have said

The face?   another story, a flag
hung upside down against glory's orders

2

Trying to think about
something else—what?—when

the story broke
the scissor-fingered prestidigitators

snipped the links of concentration
State vs memory

State vs unarmed citizen
wounded by no foreign blast nor shell

forced into the sick-field
brains-out coughing downwind

backing into the alley   hands shielding eyes
under glare-lit choppers coming through   low

3

In the dream you—is it?—set down
two packages in brown paper

saying, *Without such means*
there can be no end

to the wrenching of mind
from body, the degradation

no end to everything you hate
and have exposed, lie upon lie

I think: *We've been dying slowly*
now we'll be blown to bits

I think you're testing me
"how vitally we desired disaster"

You say, *there can be no poetry*
without the demolition

of language, no end to everything you hate
lies upon lies

I think: you're testing me
testing us both

but isn't this what it means to live—
pushing further the conditions in which we breathe?

4

In the college parlor by the fireplace
ankled and waisted with bells

he, inclined by nature toward tragic themes
chants of the eradication of tribal life

in a blue-eyed trance
shaking his neckbent silvering hair

Afterward, wine and cake at the Provost's house

and this is surely no dream, how the beneficiary
of atrocities yearns toward innocence

and this is surely a theme, the vengeful rupture
of prized familiar ways

and calculated methods
for those who were there   But for those elsewhere

it's something else, not herds hunted down cliffs
maybe a buffalo burger in the

tribal college cafeteria
and computer skills after lunch   Who wants to be tragic?

The college coheres out of old quonset huts
demolition-scavenged doors, donated labor

used textbooks, no waste, passion

5

Horned blazing fronds of Sierra ice
grow hidden rivulets, last evening's raindrop pulses

in the echeveria's cup next morning, fogdrip darkens the
    road
under fire-naked bishop pines

thick sweats form on skins
of pitched-out nectarines, dumpster shrine

of miracles of truths of mold
Rain streaming, stroking

a broken windowpane
When the story broke I thought

I was thinking about water
how it is most of what we are

and became bottled chic
such thoughts are soon interrupted

6

When the story broke we were trying to think
about history   went on stubbornly thinking

though history plunged
with muddy spurs   screamed at us for trying

to plunder its nest   seize its nestlings
capture tame and sell them or something

after the manner of our kind
Well, was it our secret hope?

—a history you could seize
(as in old folios of "natural history"

each type and order pictured in its place?)
—Back to the shambles, comrades,

where the story is always breaking
down   having to be repaired

7

Under the small plane's fast shadow an autumn
afternoon bends sharply

—swathes of golden membrane, occult blood
seeping up through the great groves

where the intestinal the intestate
blood-cords of the stags are strung from tree to tree

I know already where we're landing
what cargo we'll take on

boxed for the final draping
coming home from home   sewn into its skin

eyes hooded in refusal

—what might be due—

1998–1999

FOR THIS

If I've reached for your lines   (I have)
    like letters from the dead that stir the nerves
dowsed you for a springhead
    to water my thirst
dug into my compost skeletons and petals
    you surely meant to catch the light:

—at work in my wormeaten wormwood-raftered
    stateless underground
        have I a plea?

If I've touched your finger
    with a ravenous tongue
        licked from your palm a rift of salt
if I've dreamt or thought you
    a pack of blood   fresh-drawn
        hanging darkred from a hook
higher than my heart
    (you who understand transfusion)
        where else should I appeal?

A pilot light lies low
    while the gas jets sleep
        (a cat getting toed from stove
into nocturnal ice)
    language uncommon and agile as truth
        melts down the most intractable silence

A lighthouse keeper's ethics:
    you tend for all or none
        for this you might set your furniture on fire
A *this* we have blundered over
    as if the lamp could be shut off at will
        rescue denied for some

and still a lighthouse be

1999

REGARDLESS

An idea declared itself between us
clear as a washed wineglass
that we'd love
regardless of manifestos I wrote or signed
my optimism of the will
regardless
your wincing at manifestos
your practice of despair you named
anarchism
: : an idea we could meet
somewhere else   a road
straggling unmarked through ice-plant
toward an ocean   heartless as eternity

Still hungry for freedom   I walked off
from glazed documents   becalmed
passions   time of splintering and sawdust
pieces lying still   I was not myself but
I found a road like that   it straggled
The ocean still
looked like eternity
I drew it on a
napkin mailed it to you

On your hands you wear work gloves stiffened
in liquids your own body has expressed
: : what stiffens hardest?   tears? blood? urine? sweat? the
     first drops from the penis?
Your glove then meets my hand   this is our meeting
Which of us has gone furthest?

To meet you like this I've had to rise
from love in a room
of green leaves larger than my clitoris or my brain
in a climate where winter never precisely
does or does not engrave its name on the windowpane
while the Pacific lays down its right of way
to the other side of the world

: : to a table where singed manifestos
curl back crying to be reread

but can I even provoke you
joking or
in tears
you   in long-stiffened gloves   still
protector of despair?

for H.C.

1998–1999

SIGNATURES

It would have made no difference who commanded us in
those first hours. . . .

—veteran, invasion of Normandy, 1944

That was no country for old women . . . Someone from D-Day
at the redgold turn of the party
recites his line of Yeats with a sex-change
someone already stricken
in his urethra   rising four times nightly

Went through *that* and still despises . . .

Here an old woman's best country is her art
or it's not her country
Here the old don't pity the old
As when young we scale our rock face
relentless, avid

looking sometimes back at the whole terrain:

—those scrapings on the rocks
are they a poet's signature?
a mother's who tried for all her worth to cling
to the steep   with the small soft claws gripping her back?

1998

20

NORA'S GAZE

Clayton, we can't
    have it both ways:
        Nora's art

was erotic
    not sensual
        yet how can that be?

Mostly, she handled
    the body in a bleak light
        —surely that was her right

to make such paintings, drawings more
    than paintings anyway—
        grey-brown, black, white-grey

—not the usual hues encoding
    sensual encounter
        but how she figured it
        and stained it

And had she painted
    the deep-dyed swollen shaft
        the balls' magenta shadow

in dark dominion
    that
        might have "done well"

But to paint and paint again
    the penis as a workaday
        routine

wintry morning thing
    under a gaze
        expert and merciful as hers

that was heinous
    and her genius
        still lies chained

till that is told

    You a man
        I a woman tell it
    none of it lessens her

for Clayton Eshleman

1998

ARCHITECT

Nothing he had done before
  or would try for later
    will explain or atone
this facile suggestion of crossbeams
languid elevations traced on water
his stake in white colonnades cramping his talent
                    showing up in
facsimile mansions overbearing the neighborhood
his leaving the steel rods out of the plinths
    (bronze raptors gazing from the boxwood)

You could say he spread himself too thin   a plasterer's term
    you could say he was then
skating thin ice   his stake in white colonnades against the
  thinness of
ice itself   a slickened ground
    Could say he did not then love
his art enough to love anything more

Could say he wanted the commission so
badly betrayed those who hired him   an artist
    who in dreams followed
      the crowds who followed him

Imagine commandeering those oversize those prized
    hardwood columns to be hoisted and hung
by hands expert and steady on powerful machines
    his knowledge using theirs as the one kind does the
                    other (as it did in Egypt)

        —while devising the little fountain to run all night
        outside the master bedroom

1998–1999

FOX

I needed fox   Badly I needed
a vixen for the long time none had come near me
I needed recognition from a
triangulated face   burnt-yellow eyes
fronting the long body the fierce and sacrificial tail
I needed history of fox   briars of legend it was said she
    had run through
I was in want of fox

And the truth of briars she had to have run through
I craved to feel on her pelt   if my hands could even slide
past or her body slide between them   sharp truth distressing
    surfaces of fur
lacerated skin calling legend to account
a vixen's courage in vixen terms

For a human animal to call for help
on another animal
is the most riven the most revolted cry on earth
come a long way down
Go back far enough it means tearing and torn   endless
    and sudden
back far enough it blurts
into the birth-yell of the yet-to-be human child
pushed out of a female   the yet-to-be woman

1998

MESSAGES

I love the infinity of these silent spaces
Darkblue shot with deathrays but only a short distance
Keep of course water and batteries, antibiotics
Always look at California for the last time

We weren't birds, were we, to flutter past each other
But what were we meant to do, standing or lying down
Together on the bare slope where we were driven
The most personal feelings become historical

Keep your hands knotted deep inside your sweater
While the instruments of force are more credible than beauty
Inside a glass paperweight dust swirls and settles (Manzanar)
Where was the beauty anyway when we shouldered past
    each other

Where is it now in the hollow lounge
Of the grounded airline where the cameras
For the desouling project are being handed out
Each of us instructed to shoot the others naked

If you want to feel the true time of our universe
Put your hands over mine on the stainless pelvic rudder
No, here   (sometimes the most impassive ones will shudder)
The infinity of these spaces comforts me
Simple textures falling open like a sweater

1999

FIRE

      in the old city   incendiaries abound
who hate this place stuck to their foot soles
Michael Burnhard is being held and I
can tell you about him   pushed-out and living
across the river   low-ground given to flooding
in a shotgun house
his mother working for a hospital
or restaurant   dumpsters   she said a restaurant
hospital cafeteria who cares
what story
you bring home with the food

I can tell you Michael knows beauty
from the frog-iris in mud
the squelch of ankles
stalking the waterlily
the blues beat flung across water from the old city

Michael Burnhard in Black History Month
not his month only he was born there
not black and almost without birthday one
February 29 Michael Burnhard
on the other side of the river
glancing any night at his mother's wrists
crosshatched raw
beside the black-opal stream

Michael Burnhard still beside himself
when fire took the old city
lying like a black spider on its back
under the satellites and a few true stars

1999

TWILIGHT

Mudseason dusk schoolmaster: pressed out of rain my
   spine
on your grey dormitory
chiseled from Barre

caught now in your blurred story
hauling my jacket overshoulder
against your rectilinear stones

Out of the rain I waited
in a damp parlor ghosted
with little gifts and candy toys
pitting my brain against your will

Could rays from my pupils dissect
mortar   pry boards from floor
probe the magnetic field of your
granitic clarity

Schoolmaster: could swear I've caught your upper-window
   profile
bent down on this little kingdom   dreamed your advice:
Always read with the dark falling over your left shoulder
                             —seen you
calculate volume of blocks required
                  inspect the glazing
pay the week's wages
     blueprints scrolled under arm

treading home over snow
driven virgin then cow-pied
five o'clock's blue eyeballs
strung open day after day
a few seconds longer

an ascendant planet
following in your footprints possibly

1999

OCTOBRISH

—it is to have these dreams

still married/where
   you tell me *In those days*
            instead of working
            I was playing on the shore with a wolf

coming to a changed
house/you
glad of the changes

but still almost
transparent
and bound to disappear

      A life thrashes/half unlived/its passions
            don't desist/displaced from their own habitat
                  like other life-forms take up other dwellings

so in my body's head
so in the stormy spaces
that life
leads itself which could not be led

1999

SECOND SIGHT

1

Tonight I could write many verses
beginning   Let this not happen
for a woman leaning over a thirtieth story railing
in hot July   worn webbed-plastic
chairs aglare on the nickel-colored balcony
foreseeing in tracked patterns
of a project landscape
the hammer brought
down by one child upon another's skull

Not moved yet   she   and hers
her child inside   gazing
at a screen
and she a reader once   now a woman foreseeing

elbows sore with the weight
she has placed on them
a woman on a balcony with a child inside
gazing at a screen

2

A woman   neither architect nor engineer   construes the
    dustmotes
of a space primed for neglect
Indoor, outdoor exhausted air

Paths that have failed as paths   trees
that have failed as trees

Practiced in urban literacy she
traverses and assesses streets and bridges
tilting the cumbrous ornamental sewer lids ajar
in search of reasons underground
            which there why this must be

1999–2000

GRATING

I

Not having worn
   the pearly choker
      of innocence around my throat
willed by a woman
   whose leavings I can't afford
      Not having curled up like that girl
   in maternal gauze
              Not
   having in great joy gazing
on another woman's thick fur
   believed I was unsexed for that

Now let me not
   you   not I   but who ought to be
hang like a leaf twisting
      endlessly toward the past
     nor reach for a woman's skinned-off mask
   to hide behind
          You
               not I but who ought to be
get me out of this, human
                  through some
   air vent, grating

II

There's a place where beauty names itself:
"I am beauty," and becomes irreproachable
to the girl transfixed beside the mother
the artist and her mother

There must be a color for the mother's
otherness   must be some gate of chalk some slit or stain
through which the daughter sees outside that otherness
Long ago must have been burnt a bunch of rags
still smelling of umbrage
that can be crushed into a color
there must be such a color
if, lying full length
on the studio floor
the artist were to paint herself
in monochrome
from a mirror in the ceiling
an elongated figure suspended across the room
first horizontal

then straight up and naked
free of beauty
ordinary in fact

III

The task is to row a strong-boned, legally blind
hundred-and-one-year-old woman
across the Yangtze River

An emergency or not, depending
Others will have settled her in the boat with pillows but
    the arms
wielding the oars will be yours
crepitus of the shoulders yours
the conversation still hers

Three days' labor
*with you . . . **that** was torture*

—to pilot through current and countercurrent
requiring silence and concentration

There is a dreadfulness that charm o'erlies
—as might have been said
in an older diction

Try to row deadweight someone without
death skills

Shouldering the river a pilot figures
how

The great rock shoulders overlook
in their immensity all decisions

1999–2000

NOCTILUCENT CLOUDS

Late night on the underside   a spectral glare
abnormal   Everything below
must and will betray itself
as a floodlit truckstop out here
on the North American continent stands revealed
and we're glad because it's late evening and no town
but this, diesel, regular, soda, coffee, chips, beer and video
no government no laws but LIGHT in the continental dark
and then   and then   what smallness the soul endures
rolling out on the ramp from such an isle
onto the harborless Usonian plateau

Dear Stranger   can I raise a poem
to justice   you not here
with your sheet-lightning apprehension
of nocturne
your surveyor's eye for distance
as if any forest's fallen tree were for you
a possible hypotenuse

Can I wake as I once woke with no thought of you
into the bad light of a futureless motel

This thing I am calling justice:
I could slide my hands into your leather gloves
but my feet would not fit into your boots

Every art leans on some other: yours
on mine in spasm retching
last shreds of vanity
We swayed together like cripples when the wind
suddenly turned a corner   or was it we who turned

Once more I invite you into this
in retrospect it will be clear

1999

IF YOUR NAME IS ON THE LIST

If your name is on the list of judges
you're one of them
though you fought their hardening
assumptions   went and stood
alone by the window while they
concurred
It wasn't enough to hold your singular
minority opinion
You had to face the three bridges
down the river
your old ambitions
flamboyant in bloodstained mist

You had to carry off under arm
and write up in perfect loneliness
your soul-splitting dissent

Yes, I know a soul can be partitioned like a country
In all the new inhere old judgments
loyalties crumbling send up sparks and smoke
We want to be part of the future   dragging in
what pure futurity can't use

Suddenly a narrow street a little beach a little century
screams   *Don't let me go*

Don't let me die   Do you forget
what we were to each other

1999

1999

Before the acute
point of the severing
I wanted to see into my century's
hinged and beveled mirror
clear of smoke
eyes of coal and ruby
stunned neck the carrier of bricks and diamonds
brow of moonlit oyster shells
barbed wire lacework disgracing
the famous monument

Behind it spread the old
indigenous map   landscape
before conquerors   horizon ownless

TERZA RIMA

1

Hail-spurting sky   sun
splashing off persimmons left
in the quit garden

of the quit house   The realtor's swaying name
against this cloudheap this
surrendered acre

I would   so help me   tell you if I could
how some great teacher
came to my side and said:

Let's go down   into the underworld
—the earth already crazed
Let me take your hand

—but who would that be?
already trembling on the broken crust
who would I trust?

I become the default derailed memory-raided
limping
teacher I never had   I lead and   I follow

2

Call it the earthquake trail:
I lead through live-oak meadows
to the hillside   where the plates shuddered

rewind the seismic story
point to the sundered
fence of 1906   the unmatching rocks

trace the loop under dark bay branches
blurred with moss
behaving like a guide

Like a novice I lag
behind with the little snake
dead on the beaten path

This will never happen again

3

At the end of the beaten path we're sold free
tickets for the celebration
of the death of history

The last page of the calendar
will go up   a sheet of flame
(no one will be permitted on the bridge)

We'll assemble by letters
alphabetical
each ticket a letter

to view ourselves as giants
on screen-surround
in the parking lot

figures of men and women firmly pushing
babies in thickly padded prams
through disintegrating malls

into the new era

4

I have lost our way   the fault is mine
ours   the fault belongs
to us   I become   the guide

who should have defaulted
who should have remained the novice
I   as guide   failed

I as novice   trembled
I should have been stronger   held us
together

5

I thought I was
stronger   my will the ice-sail
speeding my runners

along frozen rivers
bloodied by sunset
thought I could be forever

will ful   my sail filled
with perfect ozone   my blades
flashing clean into the ice

6

Was that youth?   that clear
sapphire on snow
a distinct hour

in Central Park   that smell
on sidewalk and windowsill
fresh and unmixt

the blizzard's peace and drama
over the city
a public privacy

                    waiting
in the small steamed-up copy shop
slush tracked in across a wooden floor

then shivering   elated
in twilight
at the bus stop   with others   a public happiness

7

Not simple is it to do
a guide's work   the novices
irrupting hourly with their own bad vigor

knowing not who they are
every phase of moon an excuse
for fibrillating

besides the need   in today's world
to consider
outreach   the new thinking

—Or: love will strongly move you
or commerce will
You want a priest?   go to the altar

where eternal bargains are struck
want love?
go down inside your destructible heart

8

In Almodóvar's film
we go for truth to the prostitutes' field
to find past and future

elegant   beaten-up and knifed
sex without gender
preyed-on and preying

transactions   zones of play
the circling drivers
in search of their desires

theater of love   Ninth Circle
there are so many teachers
here   no fire can shrink them

Do you understand?   you could get your face
slashed in such a place
Do you think this is a movie?

9

She says: I gave my name and it was taken
I no longer have my name
I gave my word and it was broken

My words are learning
to walk on crutches
through traffic

without stammering
My name is a prisoner
who will not name names

She says: I gave my tongue
to love   and this
makes it hard to speak

She says: When my life depended
on one of two
opposite terms

I dared mix beauty with courage
they were my lovers
together they were tortured

10

Sick of my own old poems   caught
on rainshower Fifth Avenue
in a bookstore

I reach to a shelf
and there you are   Pier Paolo
speaking to Gramsci's ashes

in the old encircling rhyme
Vivo nel non volere
del tramontato dopoguerra:

                        amando
il mondo che odio . . .
that vernacular voice
intimately political

and that was how you died
so I clasp my book to my heart
as the shop closes

11

Under the blackened dull-metal corners
of the small espresso pot
a jet flares blue

a smell tinctures the room
—some sniff or prescience of
a life that actually could be

lived   a grain of hope
a bite of bitter chocolate in the subway
to pull on our senses

without them we're prey
to the failed will
its science of despair

12

How I hate it when you ascribe to me
a "woman's vision"
cozy with coffeepots   drawn curtains

or   leaning in black leather dress
over your chair
black fingernail tracing your lines

overspent Sibyl drifting in a bottle

How I've hated speaking "as a woman"
for mere continuation
when the broken is what I saw

As a woman   do I love
and hate?   as a woman
do I munch my bitter chocolate underground?

Yes.   No.   You too
sexed as you are   hating
this whole thing   you keep on   it remaking

13

Where the novice pulls the guide
across frozen air
where the guide suddenly grips   the shoulder

of the novice   where the moss is golden
the sky sponged with pink at sunset
where the urine of reindeer barely vanished

stings the air like a sharp herb
where the throat of the clear-cut opens
across the surrendered forest

I'm most difficultly
with you   I lead
and I follow

our shadows   reindeer-huge
slip onto the map
of chance and purpose   figures

on the broken crust
exchanging places   bites to eat
a glance

2000

FOUR SHORT POEMS

1

(driving home from Robin Blaser's reading)

The moon
is not romantic.   No.   It's
a fact of life and still
we aren't inured. You would think, it reflects
the waves not draws them.   So
I'd compel you as I
have been compelled by you.   On the coast road
between drafts of fog
that face (and yes, it is
expressioned) breaking in and out
doth speak to us
as he did in his courtliness
and operatic mystery.

2

We're not yet out of the everglades
   of the last century
      our body parts are still there

though we would have our minds careen and swoop
   over the new ocean
      with a wild surmise

the bloody strings
   tangled and stuck between
      become our lyre

3

Beethoven's "Appassionata" played on a parlor grand
    piano
in a small California town by a boy from Prague
here for a month to learn American
This is not "The Work of Art in the Age of Mechanical
    Reproduction"
This is one who startles the neighbors with his owning
of the transmissible heritage one evening
then for the whole month droops over the Internet.

4

From the new crudities, from the old
apartheid spraying ruin on revolution,
back to Du Bois of Great Barrington and Africa

or Kafka of the intransmissible
tradition
the stolen secrets in the cleft

reside   and this, beloved poets
is where our hearts, livers and lights still
dwell unbeknownst and vital

for Elizabeth Willis and for Peter Gizzi

2000

RAUSCHENBERG'S BED

How a bed once dressed with a kindly quilt becomes
unsleepable site of anarchy   What body holes expressed
their exaltation loathing exhaustion
what horse of night has pawed those sheets
what talk under the blanket raveled
what clitoris lain very still in her own subversion
what traveler homeward reached for familiar bedding
and felt stiff tatters under his fingers
How a bed is horizontal yet this is vertical
inarticulate liquids spent from a spectral pillow

How on a summer night someone drives out on the roads
while another one lies ice-packed in dreams of freezing

Sometimes this bed has eyes, sometimes breasts
sometimes eking forth from its laden springs
pity compassion pity again for all they have worn and borne
Sometimes it howls for penis sometimes vagina sometimes
for the nether hole the everywhere

How the children sleep and wake
the children   sleep awake upstairs

How on a single night the driver of roads comes back
into the sweat-cold bed of the dreamer

leans toward what's there for warmth
human limbs   human crust

2000

WAITING FOR YOU AT
THE MYSTERY SPOT

I sat down facing the steep place where
tours clambered upward and others straggled down, the
    redwoods outstanding all
A family, East Asian, holding a picnic at their van:
"We are always hungry," the older sister said laughing,
    "and we always bring our food"
Roses clambered a rough fence in the slanting sun that
    speared the redwoods
We'd gone into the gift shop while waiting for your tour
found Davy Crockett coonskin caps, deerskin coin purses
scorpions embedded in plastic, MYSTERY SPOT bumper
    stickers
and postcards of men you wouldn't be left alone with
a moment if you could help it, illustrating
the Mystery Spot and its tricks with gravity and horizon
Your tour was called and you started upward.   I went
    back
to my redwood bench
                "The *mystai* streamed"
                              toward the

        mystery

But if anything up there was occult
nothing at ground level was: tiny beings flashing around
in the sun secure knowing their people were nearby
grandfathers, aunts, elder brothers or sisters, parents and
    loved friends
You could see how it was when each tour was called and
    gathered itself
who rode on what shoulders, ran alongside, held hands
the languages all different, English the least of these
I sat listening to voices watching the miraculous migration
of sunshafts through the redwoods   the great spears
    folding up
into letters from the sun deposited through dark green
    slots
each one saying
                    I love you but
I must draw away   Believe, I will return

Then: happiness! your particular figures
in the descending crowd: Anne, Jacob, Charlie!
Anne with her sandals off
in late day warmth and odor and odd wonder

2000

ENDS OF THE EARTH

All that can be unknown is stored in the black screen of a
    broken television set.
Coarse-frosted karst crumbling as foam, eel eyes piercing
    the rivers.
Dark or light, leaving or landfall, male or female demarca-
    tions dissolve
into the O of time and solitude. I found here: no inter/
ruption to a version of earth so abandoned and abandoning
I read it my own acedia lashed by the winds
questing shredmeal toward the Great Plains, that ocean. My
    fear.

Call it Galisteo but that's not the name of what happened
    here.

If indoors in an eyeflash (perhaps) I caught the gazer of spaces
lighting the two wax candles in black iron holders
against the white wall after work and after dark
but never saw the hand

how inhale the faint mist of another's gazing, pacing, dozing
words muttered aloud in utter silence, gesture unaware
thought that has suffered and borne itself to the ends of
    the earth
web agitating between my life and another's?
Other whose bed I have shared but never at once together?

2000

NOTES

Again, I thank the Lannan Foundation for their encouragement and for the breadth of their vision.

The lines in Spanish in the dedication are from Violeta Parra's "Gracias a la Vida."

NORA'S GAZE

Alludes to works by the painter Nora Jaffe (1928–1994). See Clayton Eshleman, "Nora's Roar," in his *From Scratch* (Santa Rosa: Black Sparrow Press, 1998), pp. 31–49.

MESSAGES

Blaise Pascal (1623–1662): *Le silence éternel de ces espaces m'affraye.* (The eternal silence of these infinite spaces frightens me). See *Pensées of Blaise Pascal,* trans. W. F. Trotter, Everyman's Library no. 874 (London: Dent, 1948), p. 61.

MANZANAR

Site of the First War Relocation Center activated in World War II for the internment of Japanese Americans, Manzanar is located east of the Sierra Nevada range and northeast of Death Valley.

TWILIGHT

Brownington, Vermont, is the site of the "Old Stone House" completed in 1836 as a dormitory for the Orleans County Grammar School. Its architect and builder, African American Alexander Lucius Twilight, served as principal of the school for most of its existence ("The Old Stone House Museum" [Orleans, Vt.: Orleans County Historical Society, 1996]). A working granite quarry still operates in Barre, Vermont.

NOCTILUCENT CLOUDS

"Several times in the last few months, observers in the lower 48 have seen 'noctilucent clouds,' which develop about 50 miles above the earth's surface—clouds so high that they reflect the sun's rays long after nightfall. . . . [G]lobal warming seems to be driving them toward the equator. . . . In retrospect it will be clear." Bill McKibben, "Indifferent to a Planet in Pain," *New York Times,* Saturday, 4 September 1999, sec. A.

"Usonian": The term used by Frank Lloyd Wright for his prairie-inspired American architecture.

TERZA RIMA, 3

Vivo nel non volare . . . : "I live in the failed will / of the postwar time: / loving the world I hate"—Pier Paolo Pasolini, "Le Ceneri di Gramsci," in Lawrence R. Smith, ed. and trans., *The New Italian Poetry, 1945 to the Present* (Berkeley: University of California Press, 1981), pp. 80–81. See also Pier Paolo Pasolini, *Poems,* selected and trans. Norman MacAfee and Luciano Martinengo (London: John Calder, 1982), pp. 10–11.

WAITING FOR YOU AT THE MYSTERY SPOT:

"The *mystai* streamed toward [the Telestrion]." C. Kerényi, *Eleusis,* trans. Ralph Manheim, Bollingen series 65, vol. 4 (New York: Bollingen Foundation/Pantheon, 1967), p. 82.